ON THE MAP

FRANCE

Titles in This Series:

France

Italy

Spain

U.S.A.

Series editor: Daphne Butler
American editor: Marian L. Edwards
Design: M&M Partnership
Photographs: ZEFA
Map artwork: Raymond Turvey
Cover photo: *Paris*

Library of Congress Cataloging-in-Publication Data

Butler, Daphne, 1945–
   France / written by Daphne Butler.
     p.   cm. — (On the map)
   Summary: An illustrated introduction to the geography, history,
industries, people, customs, and famous landmarks of France.
   ISBN 0–8114–3675–6
   1. France — Juvenile literature. [1. France.] I. Title.
II. Series.
DC33.7.B88 1992
944–dc20   92–16648
                                         CIP
                                         AC

Typeset by Multifacit Graphics, Keyport, NJ
Printed and bound in the United States.

1 2 3 4 5 6 7 8 9 0 VH 98 97 96 95 94 93

FRANCE

Daphne Butler

RSVP
RAINTREE
STECK-VAUGHN
P U B L I S H E R S
The Steck-Vaughn Company

Austin, Texas

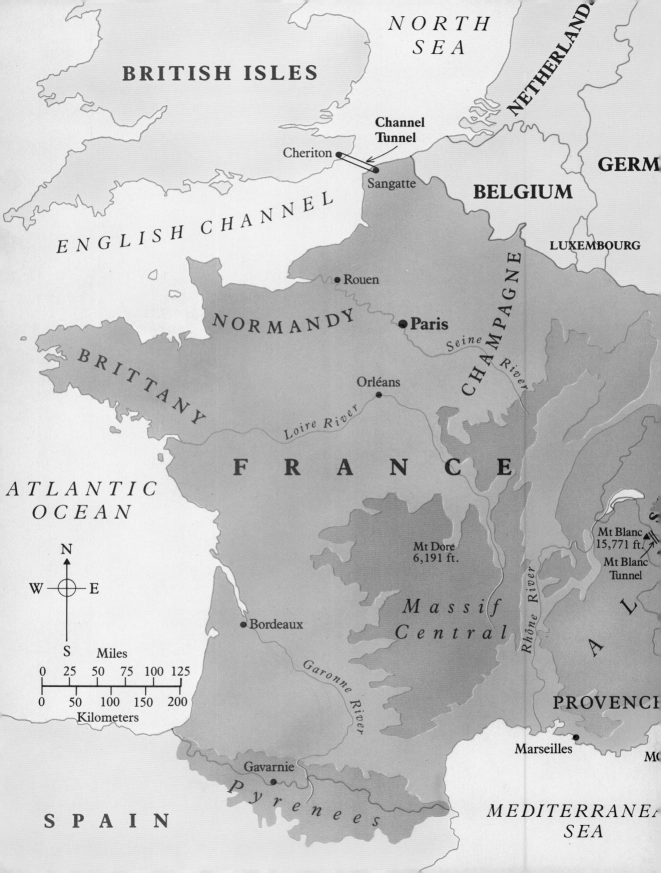

Contents

Oger in Champagne district.

Canyon du Verdun in Provence.

Mont Blanc range in Alps.

Polignac in Massif Central.

Country of Changes

France is the largest country in Europe. It is mostly bordered by water or high mountains. To the north, France is near the British Isles. The weather is mild and rainy. To the south, France joins Spain and the Mediterranean Sea. There the weather is very hot and sunny in the summer months.

The French countryside changes as you travel across it, from west to east and from north to south. In the north and west, the land has both flat and rolling plains. Sometimes the plains go for mile after mile.

The east, south, and center of the country have high hills and steep mountains. In between the mountains are deep valleys and canyons. Some of the mountains are snow-covered all year long.

Most of the northern half of France is a fertile plain. A wide variety of crops grow there. Another good farming region is in the southwest. There the grapes for France's famous wines are grown.

Much of France's low plains are separated by plateaus and mountains. However, these features are arranged in such a way that it is easy to get from one plains region to another.

Pointe du Raz facing the Atlantic Ocean.

A beach on the Mediterranean Sea at Cavaliere.

Pleherel Plage in Brittany.

On the Coast

France has coastlines on three major bodies of water. The northwest coast is on the English Channel. This waterway separates France and England. Along the coast are seaports and stretches of golden sand.

The west coast of France faces the mighty Atlantic Ocean. The tides rush in and out twice every 24 hours. The wind often blows from the west, bringing heavy storms. In some places, the jagged rocks are a serious problem for ships. Elsewhere there are sandy beaches.

The south coast of France meets the Mediterranean Sea. Because it is surrounded by land, the Mediterranean does not have very big tides. The beaches are narrow, but the sea is warm in summer. This makes it fun for swimming and other water sports. Every year visitors come to enjoy the sunbaked shores along the Mediterranean coast.

Corsica is a French island in the Mediterranean Sea. It is 106 miles southeast of the French mainland. Corsica has a long coastline with sandy beaches and palm trees. These features have made Corsica a popular vacation place for many years.

On the River

France has many small rivers that run down from the mountains towards the sea. These rivers and streams have carved deep valleys in the high mountains. Often the rivers join together, making wide waterways, deep enough for large ships to travel.

The four major rivers in France are the Loire, Rhône, Garonne, and Seine. Of these, the Loire is the longest. It rises in the Massif Central and flows westward to the Atlantic Ocean. The Garonne rises in the Pyrenees Mountains, and it too flows into the Atlantic Ocean. The Rhône, a choppy and fast-moving river, flows southward to the Mediterranean Sea. The Seine flows northwest into the English Channel that separates France from the British Isles.

Each of France's major rivers flows into one of the country's major seaports. Marseilles is the leading seaport and the second largest city in France. It is on the Mediterranean Sea. Marseilles is a great industrial and commercial center.

A system of canals connects France's main rivers with each other and with smaller rivers, too. These rivers and canals form a waterway of major importance to France's economy.

The Rhône River near Viviers.

Paris

Over 56 million people live in France. Most live in the few large towns or the many smaller towns and villages, scattered throughout the country. Paris, in the north, is on the Seine River. It is the capital and largest city in France. Paris is the headquarters for the government, the banks, and for international trade. It is a world center for art and education. About nine million people make Paris their home.

Paris is a very beautiful city. It has wide tree-lined avenues and many grand buildings. There are magnificent churches, libraries, and museums. Some of the city's buildings are hundreds of years old. Paris's museums have one of the greatest collections of art in the world. Many works of art are in the Louvre, Paris's greatest museum. The Louvre stretches for a half mile along the banks of the Seine.

The city of Paris constantly bubbles with excitement. It has long been a center for writers, artists, and musicians. It is the center of a luxury clothing industry. People all over the world follow the fashion trends set by French designers.

Each year millions of visitors come to Paris. They sightsee, shop, and eat some very good food.

Galeries Lafayette.

The Cathedral of Notre Dame.

Galeries Lafayette is probably the most famous shop in Paris. It is a big department store on the Boulevard Haussmann.

The Cathedral of Notre Dame is built on an island in the middle of the Seine River at the heart of the oldest part of the city.

La Défense is a modern business district on the northwest edge of the city. The architecture is stunning.

La Défense.

The market in St. Flour in the Massif Central is typical of markets held each day across France.

The Pattern of Life

France is a very large country. Different areas of the country have different customs, festivals, and ways of doing things. Yet, the pattern of life is much the same whatever part of France you are in.

Each town, large or small, has a square where the market is held. In small towns, market day is usually one day a week, in larger towns or cities, it is held each day.

Market day is an important day in small towns and villages. People come in from the countryside to do their shopping. They meet with their friends and relatives. Almost everything imaginable is available. There are flowers, clothing, household goods, and second-hand books. Foods range from fresh fruits, cheese, and vegetables to fish and meat. In farming areas, live farm animals are for sale.

In the large towns and busy cities, open-air or street markets are in every neighborhood. Every day before dawn sellers buy fresh produce and other goods from wholesale places. They select the freshest and best-looking items to sell in the market. Whether it is in a small town or a large one, markets are colorful and exciting places.

Families and Food

Mealtimes are at the center of family life. Parents and children try to eat all meals together as a family. Good food is an important part of everyday life in France. The people believe that good food deserves fresh ingredients, time, and attention.

Breakfast is quick and easy. Often it is bread with jam and hot chocolate or coffee. The coffee is served in a wide two-handled bowl for dipping the bread.

Lunch begins shortly after twelve o'clock noon. For most French people lunch is the main meal of the day. In many parts of the country, everything stops for two hours or longer. Shops and businesses close, and children leave school. Many people go home for lunch. Still others crowd into restaurants or one of the many eating places in France. Lunch is sometimes three or more courses. The meal might begin with appetizers, then meat and vegetables, followed by dessert or fruit.

In the evening dinner is eaten around eight o'clock. It is a lighter meal than lunch. There might be soup followed by meat or fish and salad, followed by cheese and fruit. There is always bread, water, and maybe local wine for the adults.

There are many restaurants in France serving good inexpensive food.
People often eat outside when the weather is warm.

Going to School

In France children must go to school when they are six years old. From age two to six, children can attend nursery school. Education is free and is run by the French government. All schools open at the same time and teach similar lessons. Some children in France attend private schools run by the Catholic Church.

School starts at eight o'clock in the morning and closes at four in the afternoon. Children have a two-hour lunch period. Many go home to eat lunch with their families. After school there is homework, even for the youngest children. School is closed on Wednesday, but open half a day on Saturday. Each summer all schools are closed for two and a half months.

Students have five years of elementary school followed by four years of junior high. After junior high, they can go to a general high school or vocational high school. Vocational schools offer job training in business, farming, crafts, and various kinds of industry. General high school provides three-year courses to prepare students for universities.

At the end of general high school, students must take a hard test. Those students who pass the test can enter a university of their choice.

These pictures show typical elementary school classrooms.
Most schools do not have uniforms.

Traffic in Orléans.

Traffic on the Périphérique, the road around Paris.

The TGV is the fastest train in the wor

Getting Around

You can travel around France very easily by car, train, or plane. Paris is at the center, and highways and railroads stretch out to all parts of the country. The French government makes sure that the highways and railroads are looked after and improved.

France has one of the best railroad systems in the world. The TGV (Train Grande Vitesse) is a high speed train. It is the fastest train in the world and can reach a speed of 235 miles an hour. The trains are modern and comfortable. They are sound-proofed, air conditioned, and equipped with telephones. The TGV links Paris with cities in the west and south of France.

Traffic is very heavy in France's cities. Many people use bicycles to get around. The countryside is suitable for biking too. The wide roads and flat or rolling land makes biking enjoyable. Bicycles can be rented in most towns and villages and at railroad stations.

In the past, the French took vacations in July and August. This caused the roads to the south of France to be jammed with cars. In recent years, vacation dates have changed and more people go either earlier or later.

Work and Industry

People in France are early risers. They start work between seven and eight o'clock in the morning. After a two- to three-hour lunch, they return to work until about seven in the evening.

French people seem to have a knack for keeping the best of the old ways and combining them with new ideas. They like things to look good and work well, but they are not afraid to try something new. In this way, France has become a successful industrial nation. Its goods and services are sold all over the world.

Factories in French towns and cities produce steel, chemicals, and textiles. French clothing, perfume, and cosmetics are big business. Cheese and chocolate are shipped to other countries.

The car and aircraft industries are especially important. The country is the world's fourth leading maker of cars. The French also build electronic machines such as computers and televisions.

Large mineral deposits provide French factories with the resources they need. Deposits of energy fuels, such as coal and natural gas, are important. Swift-flowing rivers from the Alps give France hydroelectric power.

Traditional crafts flourish
throughout France.

Paris is a very important
fashion center.

Making medicines has become an
important new industry.

Computer technology helps industry
to be more effective.

Sunflowers are grown for the oil in their seeds.

Peaches are packed carefully for market.

Oysters are farmed on the Atlantic coast.

Grapes are picked by machine in October

Flowers are grown for the perfume industry.

Dairy cattle provide m yogurt, butter, and che

Farming

There are farms all over France. More than ninety percent of the land is fertile. The fertile soil produces much more food than France needs for its people. The country exports a large amount of grains, wine, and potatoes to other places.

Because of the way the weather changes from north to south, farmers are able to grow many different kinds of crops. In the north farmers raise dairy cattle and grow sugar beets, apples, and pears.

Going southward, there are vast fields of wheat, barley, potatoes, and golden sunflowers. The sunflowers are grown for their oil.

In the south it is warm enough to grow peaches, apricots, nectarines, and flowers for perfume. All over the country there are vineyards. France produces some of the best wines in the world. Around the coasts, fish and shellfish are farmed.

France has few large farms. Most farms are small and are owned by the farmers. Some farms are just small plots and strips of land. Many French farmers live in towns and villages. They go out to the fields each morning and return home at night.

Leisure Time

Cafes in every town and village provide a meeting point for friends and families. Summer afternoons and evenings are often the time for a game of boules. The game is played much like bowling. Every town has a shady area set aside for playing boules.

The French believe in looking after their health and staying in shape. Exercising and playing sports is very popular with the people. Walking and hiking is enjoyed by all ages. So are jogging, swimming, tennis, and bicycling. Most weekends are devoted to these activities.

The people of France love to watch sports. The Tour de France bicycle race is one of the main sporting events of the year. Millions of people watch this event live or on television. The most popular team sport is soccer. Every region has its own team.

People usually take vacations in July and August. All French workers get five weeks vacation each year. Families head for the mountains or for the Mediterranean coast. Many city people have second homes in the country. They like to spend weekends and holidays at their country homes.

Cafés provide a meeting place for friends and families.

Learning to sail in Brittany

Swimming lessons begin at an early age

Boules is played throughout France

Famous Landmarks

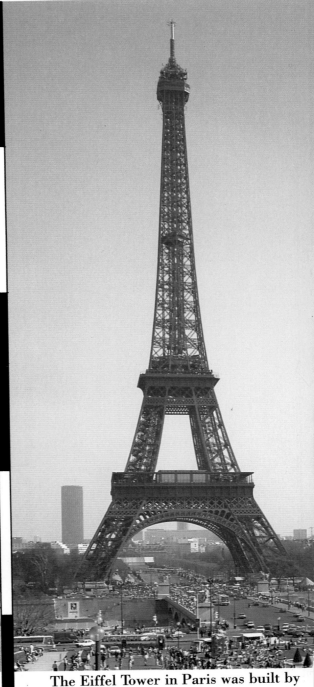

The old town of Rouen, in the west of France, where Joan of Arc was burned as a witch by the English in 1431.

The Eiffel Tower in Paris was built by Gustave Eiffel for the Universal Exhibition of 1889.

The Arc de Triomphe at the end of the Champs Élysées in Paris was built in memory of Napoleon's victories.

The Pont du Gard was built by the Romans 2,000 years ago to carry the water supply to the city of Nîmes.

The painter Claude Monet planted a beautiful garden at his house in Giverny near Rouen.

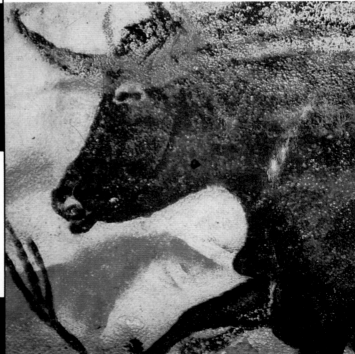

The black bull in the Lascaux caves is thousands of years old and was painted in prehistoric times.

Facts and Figures

France-the Land and People

Number of people:	about 56,000,000
Area of land:	about 210,026 sq. mi.
Size:	about 590 mi. north to south about 605 mi. east to west
Capital city: Number of people:	Paris about 8,700,000
Language:	French
Religion:	mostly Roman Catholic but all major religions practiced

Major Public Holidays

January 1	New Year's Day
date varies	Easter Monday
May 1	Labor Day
May 8	VE Day (1945)
date varies	Ascension Day (40 days after Easter)
date varies	Pentecost (7th Monday after Easter)
July 14	Bastille Day (1789)
August 15	The Assumption
November 1	All Saints' Day
November 11	Armistice Day (1918)
December 25	Christmas Day

Hours and Money

School hours:	8:00 A.M. to 4:00 P.M. Mondays, Tuesdays, Thursdays, Fridays 10:00 A.M. to 12:00 P.M. Saturdays (2 hours for lunch)
Shopping and business hours:	8 A.M. to 7:00 P.M. (2–3 hours for lunch)
Money:	French francs (FF) 1FF is about .18 (1 franc = 18 cents)

Landmarks

Highest mountain:	Mont Blanc in the Alps 15,771 ft.
Longest river:	Loire River 620 miles
Longest waterfall:	Gavarnie in the Pyrénées 1,390 ft.
Mont Blanc tunnel:	7.1 miles from Chamonix to Courmayeur in Italy
Channel tunnel:	31 miles from Sangatte near Calais to Cheriton near Folkestone in Britain

Average Temperatures in Fahrenheit

	January	July
Paris (north)	37°F	64°F
Bordeaux (west)	41°F	68°F
Nice (south)	46°F	75°F

French National Anthem: "La Marseillaise"—composed 1792 as a marching song for French troops.

Further Reading

Fiction

Carlson, Natalie S. *Happy Orpheline*. Harper Collins Children's Books, 1957.

Birchman, David F. *Victorious Paints the Great Balloon*. Macmillan Children's Book Group, 1991.

Lear, Edward and DePaola, Tomie. *Bonjour, Mister Satie*. Putnam, 1991.

Non-Fiction

Bailey, Donna and Sproule, Anna. *France*. Steck-Vaughn, 1990.

Grisewood, John. *Fun to Learn French*. Franklin Watts, 1992.

James, Ian. *France*. Watts, 1989.

Moss, Peter and Palmer, Thelma. *France*. Childrens, 1986.

Norbrook, Dominique. *Passport to France*. Watts, 1986.

Audio-Visuals

Audio Cassettes

Mahoney, Judy. *Teach Me French*. Teach Me Tapes, Inc., Minneapolis, MN, 1985.

Videotapes

Spot's First View. 30 min. Gessler Publishing, NY, 1990.

Index